THE WIND EAGLE

A Native American Folk...
retold by Joyce McGre...
Illustrated by David McCall ...

HAMPTON-BROWN

Once, at the dawn of day,
Gluscabi went fishing for salmon.
He sang his fishing song:
   noo-lin-too
   noo-lin-too.

The morning breeze grew into an angry wind that shoved Gluscabi back to shore. Gluscabi roared, "Wind from the mountains! Quiet down! I want to fish!"

But the wind didn't listen. So Gluscabi decided
to climb the mountain and stop the wind.

As he climbed, the fierce wind forced him
to crawl like a wounded wolf. Still he climbed.

The wind rose up and struck
Gluscabi down. He had to drag
himself like a sickly snake.
Still he climbed.

Finally Gluscabi reached the mountaintop, where he saw the Wind Eagle. With each beat of the eagle's powerful wings, a giant wind rushed over the land.

"Eagle!" Gluscabi wailed. "Your wind has grown too strong. Send a young breeze, warm and soft as a whispered secret." But the Wind Eagle refused, for it was far too proud of its power.

A great rage came over Gluscabi. He glared at the proud eagle and knew what he had to do.

"Eagle!" Gluscabi shouted. "Come close so that I can see your beautiful feathers."

Filled with pride, the eagle strutted toward Gluscabi. As it passed a crevice, Gluscabi shoved the eagle down inside. Its mighty wings could no longer flap.

The next morning Gluscabi returned to
the lake. He fished all day and sang with joy:
   noo-lin-too
   noo-lin-too.

And the next morning and the next, Gluscabi
fished and sang.

But as the days passed, the air became heavy. The lake turned still and dark.

The salmon began to die.

The people of the
village started to suffer.

Gluscabi cried, "It is I who caused the wind to stop. Now I must see that it blows over our land again."

So Gluscabi climbed the mountain again.

When he reached the crevice, he called,
"Eagle! I will free you if you promise to send
only gentle winds."

After a silence, the Wind Eagle answered, "I promise."

When Gluscabi set the eagle free, it began to flap its wings slowly, very slowly.

That is why today we have gentle winds.
But sometimes the Wind Eagle forgets its
promise. And then fierce winds, hurricanes,
and cyclones roar over the land.